WHAT IS

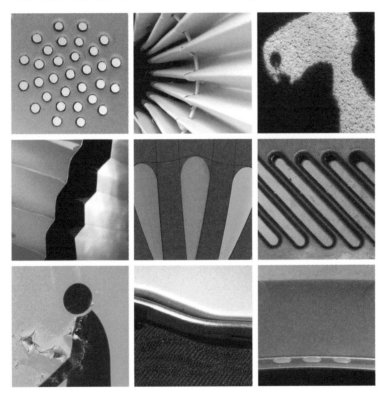

OVER 200 PICTURE PUZZLES

by

WHAT IS IT?

Published in Great Britain and USA by
AAPPL Artists' and Photographers' Press Ltd.
Church Farm House, Wisley, Surrey, GU23 6QL, UK
info@aappl.com   www.aappl.com

Sales and Distribution
UK and export: Turnaround Publisher Services Ltd.   orders@turnaround-uk.com
USA and Canada: Sterling Publishing Inc. NY   sales@sterlingpub.com
Australia: Peribo Pty Ltd.   michael.coffey@peribo.com.au

Originally published in hardback by AAPPL 2005
Copyright this paperback edition © AAPPL Artists' and Photographers' Press Ltd. 2007
Photographs copyright © Ditz   ditz@aappl.com

A catalogue record for this book is available from the British Library.

ISBN 978-1-904332-75-6   1-904332-75-7

Art Director: Ditz   ditz@aappl.com
Design: Niki Nekuda   office@nekuda.at

Printed in Malaysia by: Imago Publishing   info@imago.co.uk

WHAT IS IT?

OVER 200 PICTURE PUZZLES

it's the photographer in a bathroom
...but they won't all be this easy...

the shadow of pets playing in a sunny room

an old bird cage

an echinacea

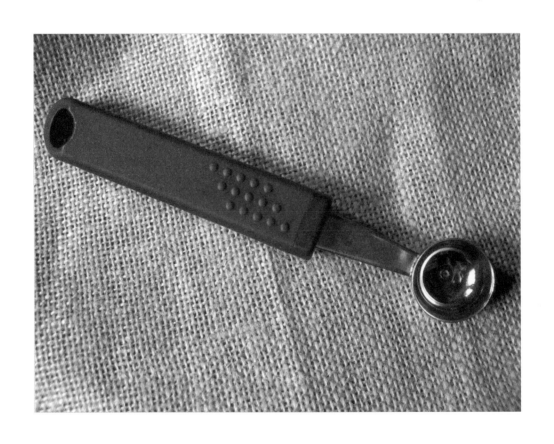

a melon-baller

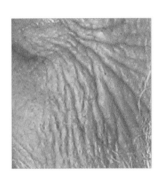

Terry's laughter lines

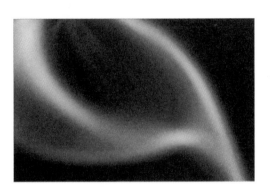

opposite page: cigarette smoke

making charcoal

a red poppy

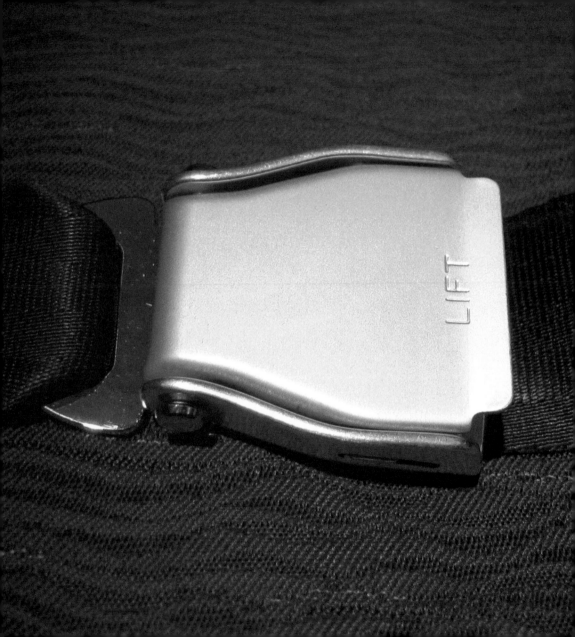

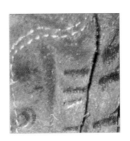

opposite page: a seatbelt buckle on a plane

one used right boot

a cowboy's boot in the stirrup

a dog on his sofa

a pair of pinking-shears

a cowboy's lasso

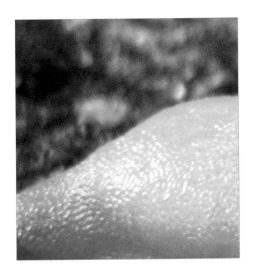

opposite page: an old sweet chestnut

a rather large slug

a dome on a bouncy castle

opposite page: a climbing wall

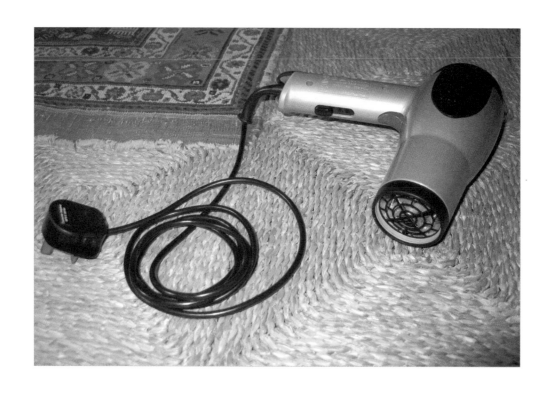

a hairdryer

opposite page: blackberries

opposite page: hamburgers on an open grill

a protective grill on a ranch pick-up truck

opposite page: a heron

raindrops on a mountain ash

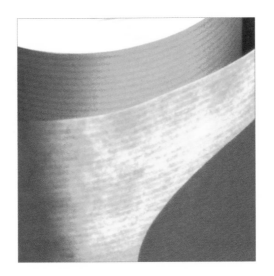

a roll of brown wrapping-paper

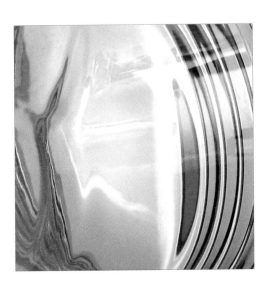

opposite page: the door of a washing machine

icicles

opposite page: a finial on a roof

a pair of kitchen scissors

opposite page: an outside staircase

opposite page: a tree-fungus

a cauliflower

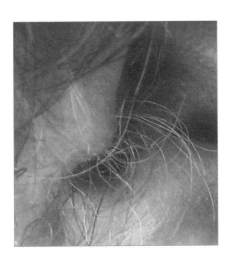

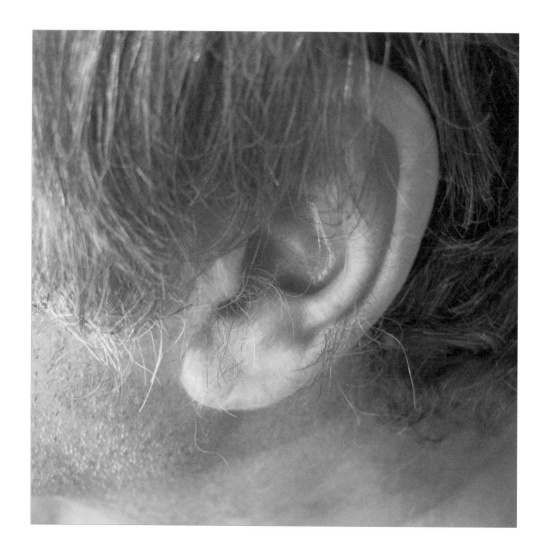

opposite page: a very hairy ear

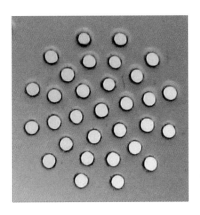

opposite page: a drummer

a colander

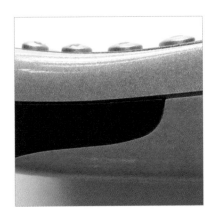

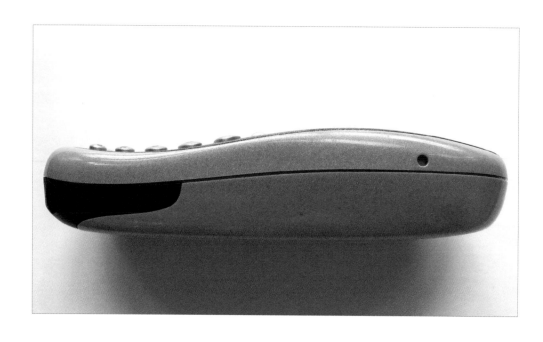

a phone

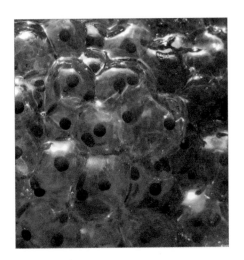

opposite page: frogspawn

the muzzle of a llama

opposite page: a lady's curly hair

a lamp in a motel bedroom

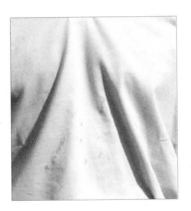

opposite page: a children's slide at a fair

opposite page: the Prince of Wales' polo shirt

ceiling lights in an amusement arcade

opposite page: a windmill

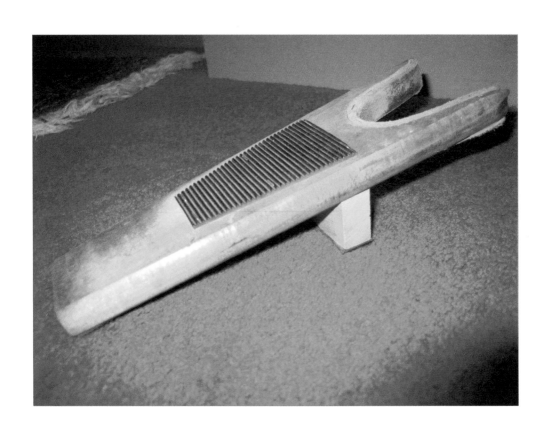

a boot-jack

opposite page: a telescope

bobbies at the fair

a lady up a ladder

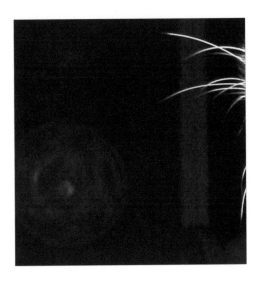

opposite page: acorns

opposite page: the cat's whiskers

a tranquilising gun

a boy-eating tiger at a fair

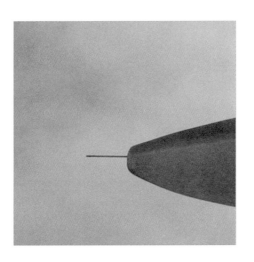

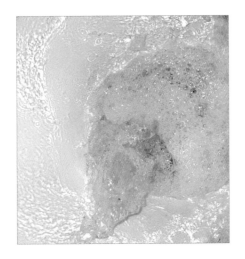

opposite page: an antenna on a plane's wing

a toilet being flushed

a cowpat

opposite page: distortion through a tumbler

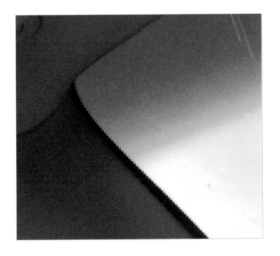

opposite page: a yellow poppy

a car windshield

a children's roundabout

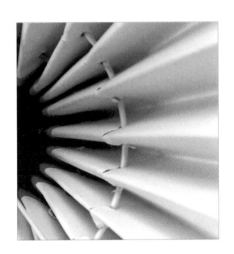

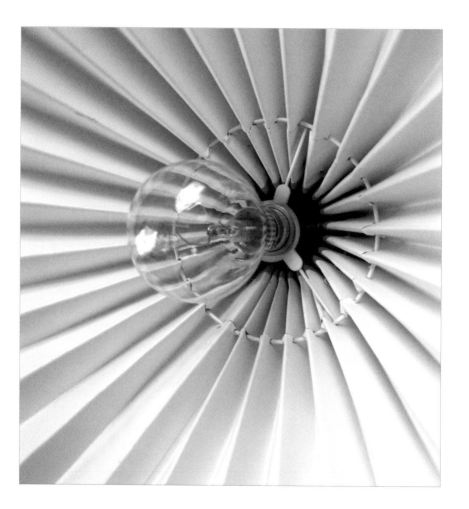

opposite page: a lampshade

a champagne-bottle stopper

opposite page: an iron stove

opposite page: a flowerpot

a watering-can

a froglet

opposite page: a robin

an ornamental garden

a toadstool

a goat's skull

opposite page: a shot road sign

dirty jeans

an old home-made sledge

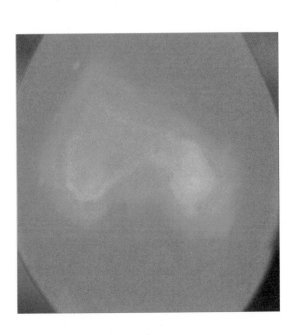

rose-hips

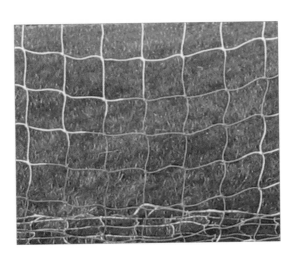

a goal

opposite page: a girl's hair

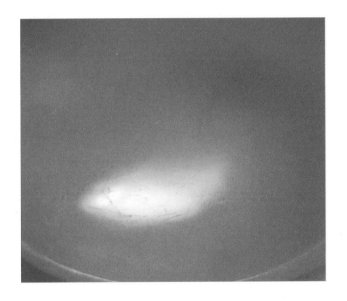

opposite page: a rocking-chair

measuring-spoons

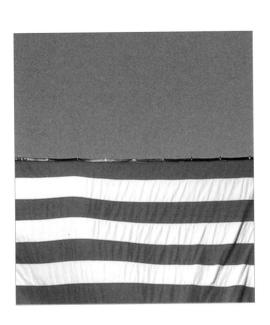

the American flag

opposite page: a guitar player

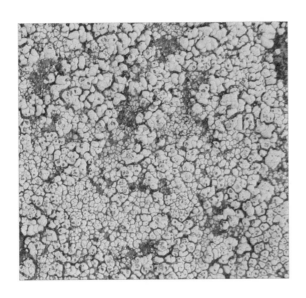

opposite page: the guardsman's busby

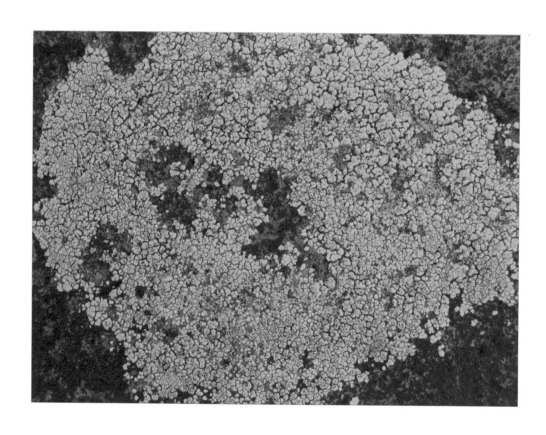

lichen on a rock

opposite page: an eggwhisk

a rosebud

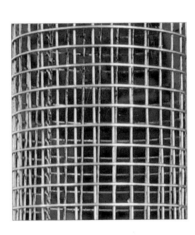

a bird-feeder

opposite page: a curious wooden bear

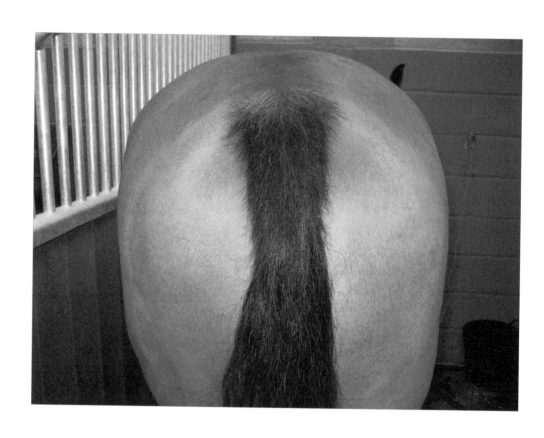

a horse's behind

a fan

a cloud at sunset

lights on a truck's roof

a fish slice

a hole-punch

opposite page: a very small, very red mushroom

the protective sheath on a cable

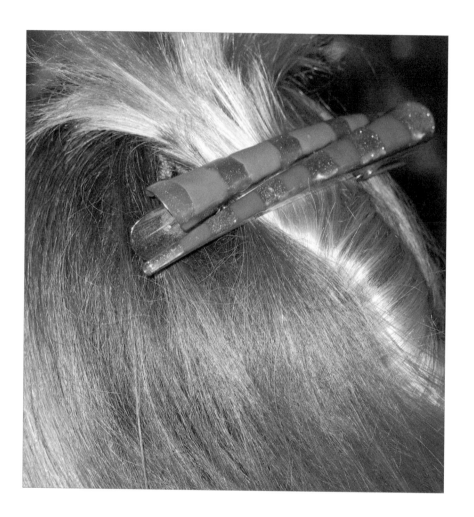

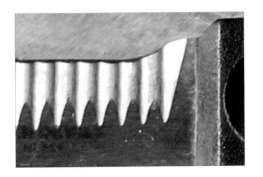

opposite page: hair-clips

a pair of scissors

a snail on a flowerpot

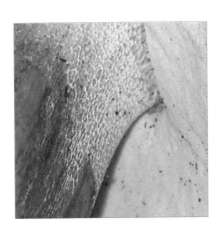

a pair of edible mushrooms

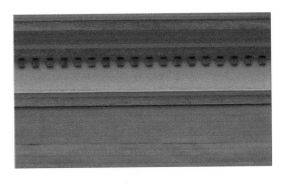

an old saloon

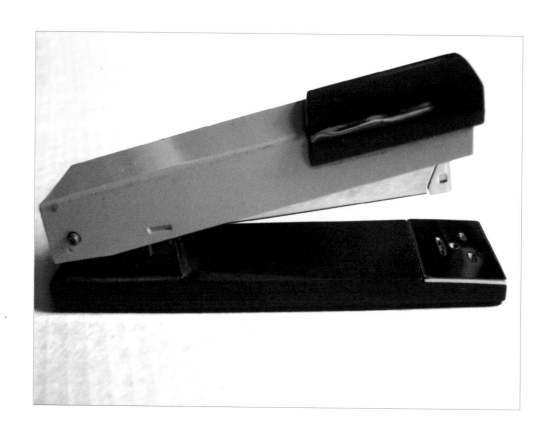

a stapler

one soft roll...

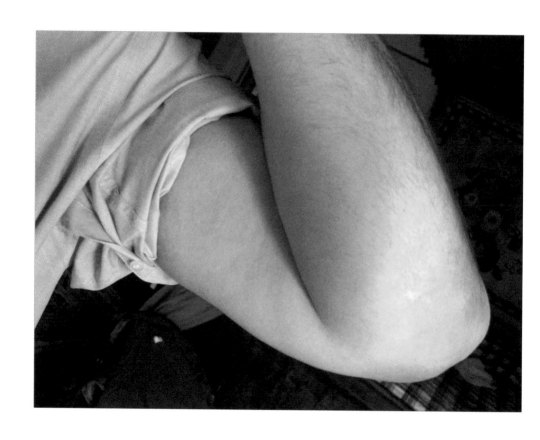

...not what you thought...

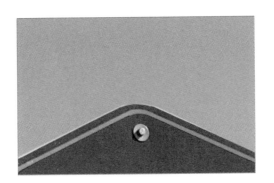

opposite page: a roadsign

an upside-down snail

opposite page: a Canada goose

opposite page: a country road

spectacles in their case

reflections of dodgems at a fair

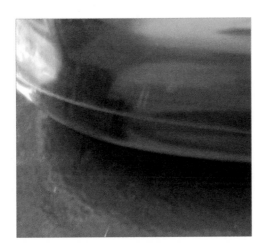

a computer-mouse

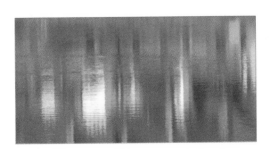

reflections in a pond

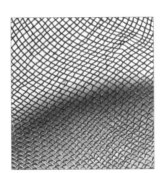

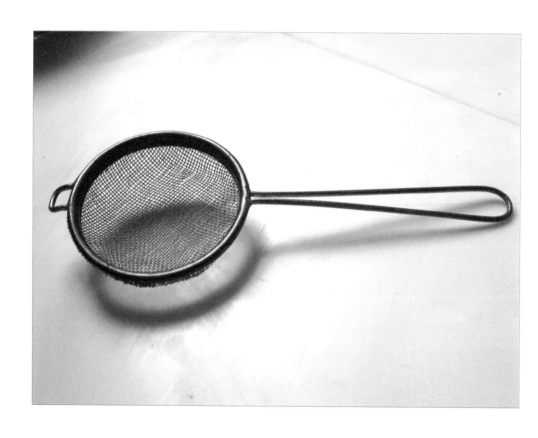

a tea-strainer

a tractor

a door-chain

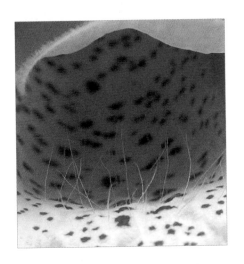

opposite page: a pair of tassels

a foxglove

opposite page: a duck's calling card

a potato-masher

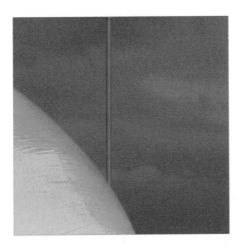

opposite page: snowy trees at night

the roof of a fairground attraction

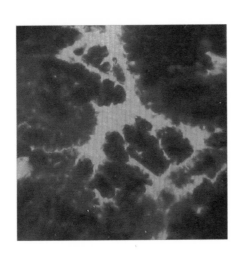

opposite page: the pickguard of a guitar

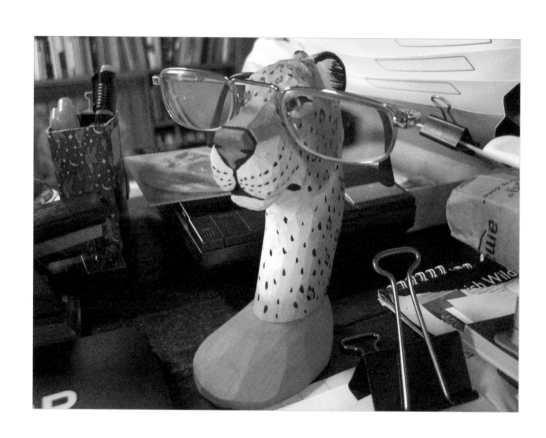

spectacles on their stand

opposite page: the cat's ear

the robin's foot

a narrow-gauge railway trestle

a piglet

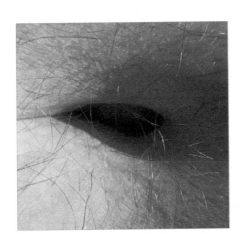

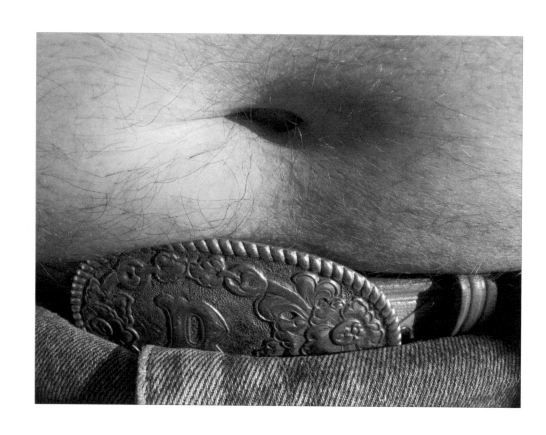

a belly button

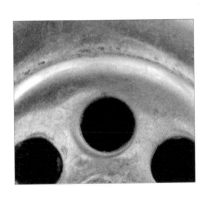

the overflow in an old bathtub

opposite page: a cygnet

the shadow of horses and riders

an old broom

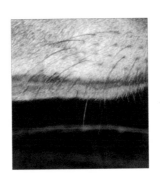

a whippet's mouth

making candyfloss

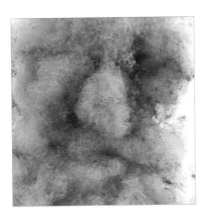

opposite page: insects on iris leaves

opposite page: an old bulrush

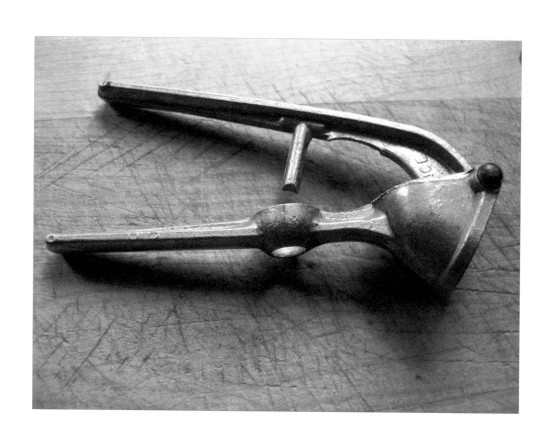

a cherry stoner/garlic press

an old lantern

a duck's legs in a puddle

a desk lamp

living statues

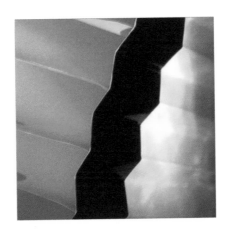

opposite page: a melon

a concertina file

a book of matches

a swan

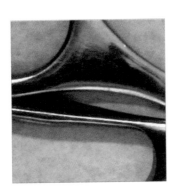

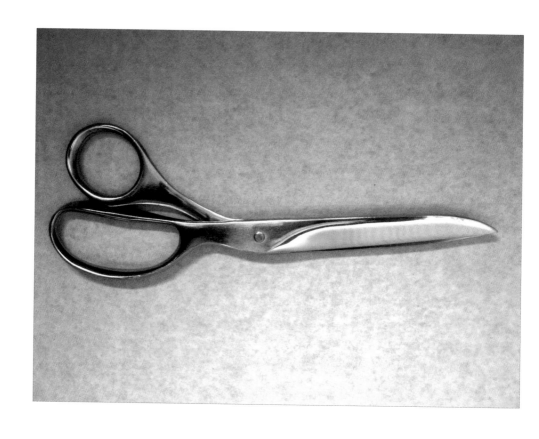

a pair of dressmaking-scissors

a helicopter

opposite page: a poly-tunnel

an ink bottle

an old cut log

Wiener schnitzel

a swallow's wings

opposite page: hoofprints in a rodeo arena

a plate of Mexican food

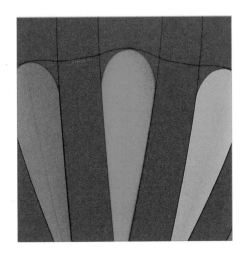

opposite page: red roses

a hot-air balloon

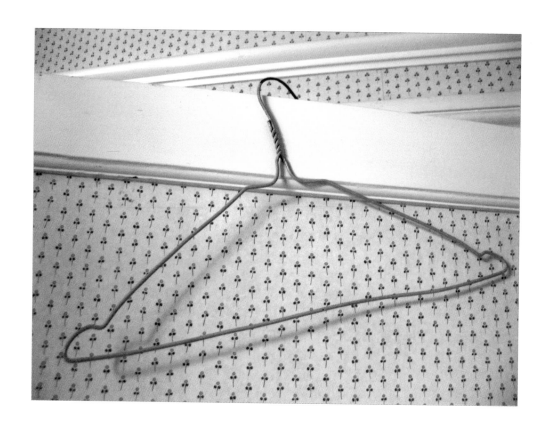

a wire coat-hanger

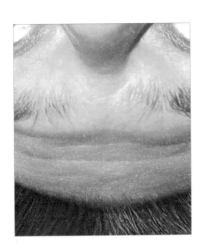

the photographer's brother

the step of an old steam-train

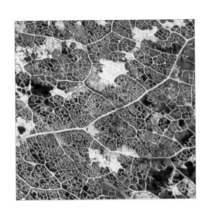

a decomposing leaf

a cowboy hat and truck

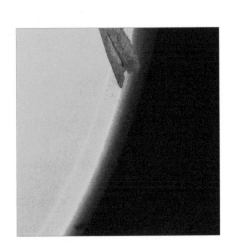

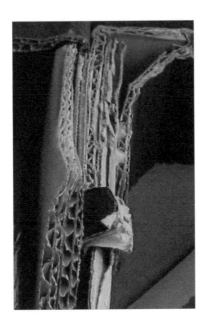

opposite page: a small moth on a lampshade

a cardboard box

opposite page: hungry caterpillars

a house on the move

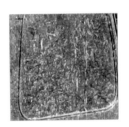

opposite page: a letter-box

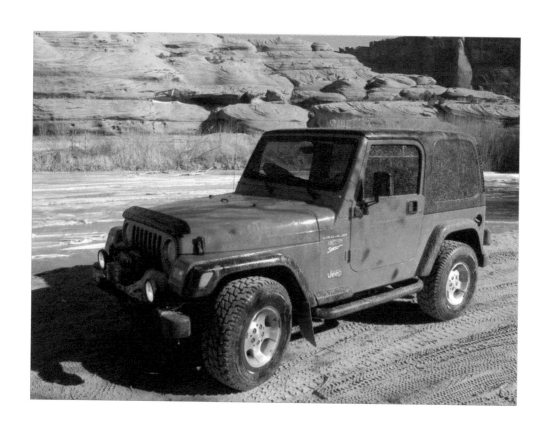

a dirty car-window

a garden table in winter

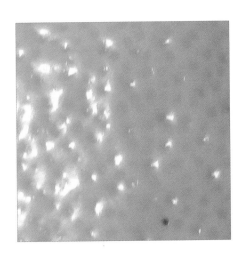

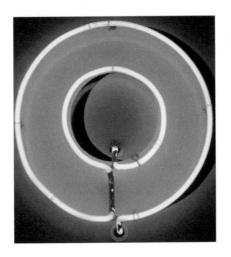

opposite page: a lemon

a neon sign

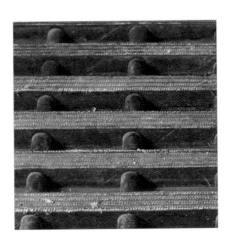

a doormat

lichen on a branch

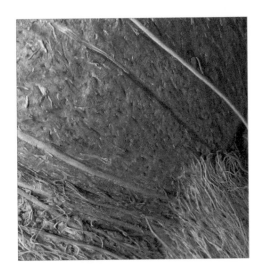

opposite page: a coyote in the snow

a coconut

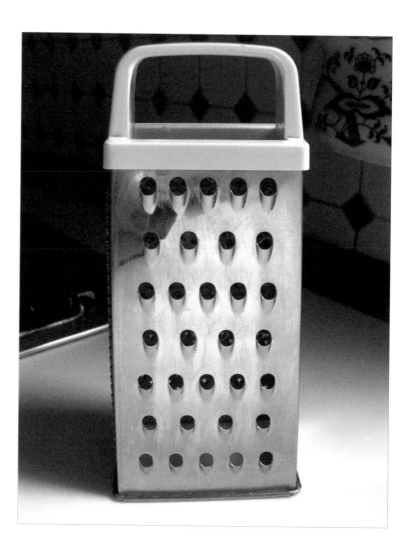

opposite page: a cheese-grater

an eroded hill

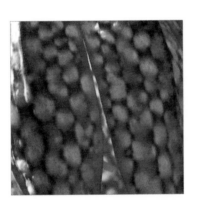

a fritillary

an old pick-up truck

a plug

algae in a stream

young fir-cones

opposite page: an ambulance at a horse show

a kitchen-towel

an apple-corer

opposite page: the door frame of house number 108 ½

opposite page: a one-man band

glasses in an old bar

a millrace

a roll of bubble-wrap

a dimmer switch

a silver birch

the raven's beak

street acrobats

kitchen foil

opposite page: a shaving-brush

a cupboard handle

an old fruit-press

distant rain at sunset

opposite page: a cobweb

opposite page: a cotton reel

young sweetcorn

the image in the wing-mirror of a pick-up truck

the horse's mouth

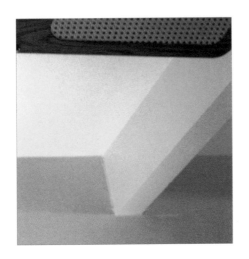

a ceiling fan

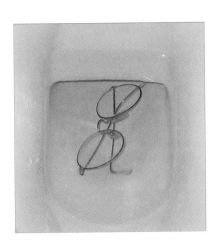

oops!

a crow's skull

work on the design of this book

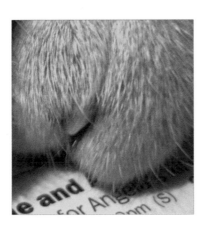

a cat's toes

a thousand thanks to Niki

who made the book look just like I thought it should

Dift